EASTON AREA PUBLIC LIB.

3 1901 0023 4552

NO LONGER PROPERTY
OF EASTON AREA
PUBLIC LIBRARY

P9-AQJ-215

NO LONGER PROPERTY
OF EASTON AREA
PUBLIC LIBRARY

Thank You Very Much, Captain Ericsson!

by Connie Nordhielm Wooldridge

illustrated by Andrew Glass

EASTON AREA PUBLIC LIBRARY
515 CHURCH STREET
EASTON PA 18042-3587

Holiday House / New York

Captain John Ericsson was a Swedish-born engineer and inventor. When he wasn't busy succeeding, he was busy failing . . . *gloriously.*

Sometimes his failures were his own fault. But more often the fault was in the eyes of those who looked at his inventions and couldn't manage to see out of the present and into the possible.

Take the fire engine he invented in 1828 when he left Sweden and went to live in England. **What a beauty it was:** sleek and efficient, with a steam-powered boiler. It could shoot gallons of water as high as ninety feet.

But such a *quantity* of water, complained the London Fire Brigade.
Surely such a deluge would cause mischief. They were perfectly
content to sprinkle fires with hand pumps and pray for rain.

"No. We'll not be needing your steam fire engine, thank you very much, Captain Ericsson," sniffed the London Fire Brigade.

So in 1829 John designed a steam locomotive, the *Novelty*, which he
built in seven weeks and entered in a race called the Rainhill Trials.
Clutching his top hat in one hand and the guardrail with the other,
he flew down the tracks at the death-defying speed of thirty miles per hour.

But the directors of the Liverpool and Manchester Railway trembled as they watched. ***Was such speed advisable? Was it healthy?*** They much preferred safety, security, and slower-moving scenery. On its last run, the *Novelty*'s engine faltered. The directors of the Liverpool and Manchester Railway heaved sighs of relief and awarded the prize to a slower engine.

"**No.** We'll not be needing your steam locomotive, thank you very much, Captain Ericsson," they told him.

So in 1837 John attached the screw propeller he'd just invented to a tugboat and demonstrated how efficient it was by towing the very starched lords of the Admiralty down the river Thames in their very proper barge.

But the lords of the Admiralty preferred the familiar splash
of the paddle wheel. You could *see* a paddle wheel.
    You could know precisely that the paddle wheel was moving the boat.
    There was something highly suspicious about this newfangled screw
propeller that did its work underwater, out of sight, and silently.

"No. We'll not be needing your screw propeller,
thank you very much, Captain Ericsson,"
declared the lords of the Admiralty.

The British decided John Ericsson had a *screw loose*.

John decided he was ready for a new place, with new eyes.
So when an American acquaintance, Captain Robert F. Stockton,
suggested he design a warship for the United States Navy,
John Ericsson sailed across the Atlantic Ocean to New York City.

The wooden warship he created upon his arrival was called the *Princeton*. The *Princeton* was fast, turned on a dime, and was outfitted with newly designed guns. The navy brass recognized it as a work of genius, and their admiration caused Captain Stockton, as commanding officer, to forget the inventor completely and bask in the praise for this fantastic ship all by himself.

That is, until some very important people were touring the ship and a gun **(which was practically the only thing Stockton *had* designed)** suddenly exploded. The disaster brought the inventor's name back to Stockton's mind. Stingy about sharing the praise, he was more than willing to share the blame. John Ericsson was never paid for his work on the *Princeton,* and he vowed he would have nothing more to do with the United States Navy.

For almost twenty years, he kept that vow.
But after the Civil War began, a man named Cornelius Bushnell
knocked on the door of John's New York home, wanting to show him something.
It was a model of an ironclad ship the North wanted to build.

According to Mr. Bushnell, the South was at work on its own ironclad
and meant to use it to break the blockade the North had set up.
Unless the Ironclad Board appointed by President Lincoln
could come up with something to challenge the South's ironclad,
the North's flimsy wooden ships would be reduced to matchsticks,
the blockade would be broken, and the Confederates would be able to ship
in the guns and supplies they needed to keep fighting.

Would John Ericsson examine Mr. Bushnell's model
to see if it would be stable enough to float?

The inventor in John Ericsson couldn't resist taking a look. He assured Mr. Bushnell the model ship would float if built. Then John showed Mr. Bushnell an ironclad model of his own that he had designed years before.

As soon as he laid eyes on it, Mr. Bushnell realized John Ericsson's model was exactly the thing the Union navy needed to hold the blockade. He hurried back to Washington to show the Ironclad Board John's model, and he convinced the inventor to follow him a few days later.

But when John arrived, the Ironclad Board greeted him with the same words he'd heard too many times before.

"No. We'll not be needing your ironclad ship, thank you very much, Captain Ericsson."

By this time, John Ericsson had had quite enough of rejection, thank you very much. He demanded to know the board's objections to his design. He answered every one of those objections with such confidence and brilliance that the board members had the uncomfortable feeling that *not* building Ericsson's ironclad amounted to an act of sheer stupidity.

"Gentlemen," John concluded, "I consider it your duty to your country to give me an order to build this vessel before I leave this room."

The order was given. A contract was signed. One hundred one working days later, the USS *Monitor* was launched.

The South's ironclad, the *Merrimac,* was hard about the business of sinking Union ships at Hampton Roads, Virginia, when, on March 9, 1862, the *Monitor* arrived on the scene. If the *Monitor* could stop the destruction and hold the blockade, the tide of the war would turn.

But no clear-thinking onlooker would have bet money on the strange-looking little *Monitor*. The *Merrimac* was four times her size and carried ten guns to her two. It was sure the *Merrimac* would swat the *Monitor* away like a bothersome fly and then finish off the Union fleet.

But the *Merrimac*'s size made her slow and clumsy and afraid of low tides and shallow waters. Most of the *Monitor* floated below the waterline, which meant there was little for the *Merrimac* to aim her guns at. The two ironclads battled for four and a half furious hours until the *Merrimac*, leaking a bit and low on fuel, hauled off.

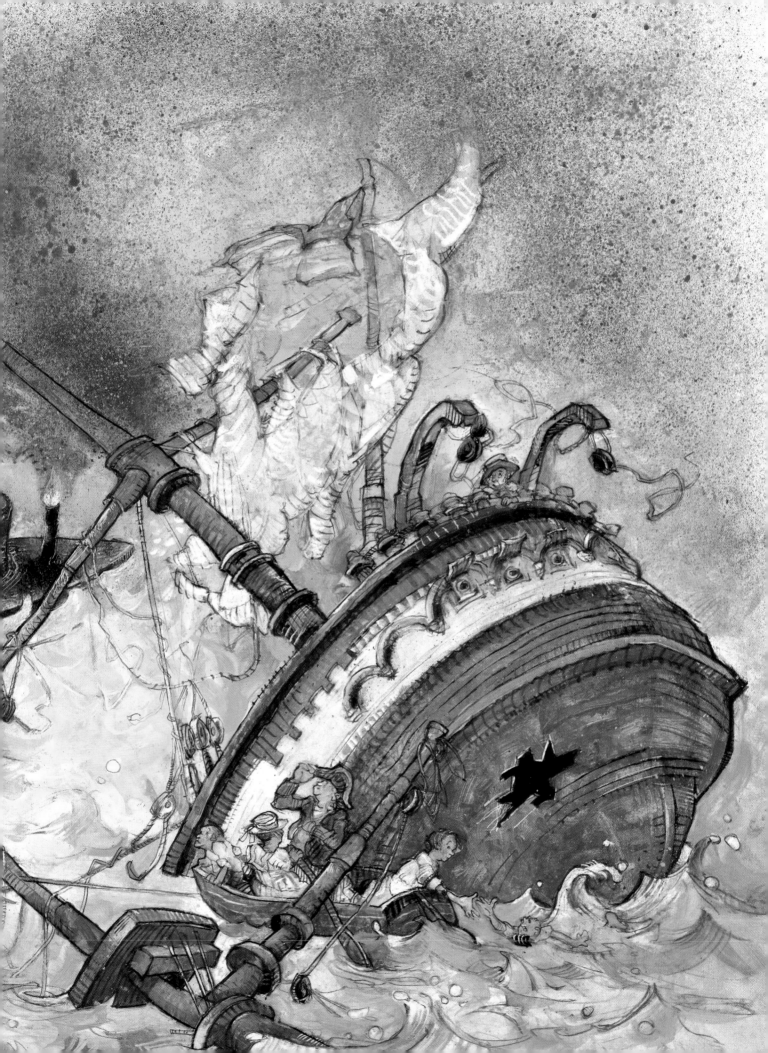

Both ships claimed victory. Only slightly damaged herself, the *Merrimac* had sunk one of the Union's ships and burned another before the *Monitor* arrived. Surely she was the winner of the battle.

But the North had a different view. The North insisted that victory was not determined by number of ships sunk but by which side reached its larger military goal. By that measure, the Union's *Monitor* was clearly the victor: The blockade held, saved by John Ericsson's crazy-looking "cheese box on a raft," his "tin can on a shingle." The South's supply line through Chesapeake Bay was choked off at Hampton Roads. The inventor with a screw loose was a hero.

John Ericsson kept his eyes fixed on the possible and cranked out invention after invention until he died at the age of eighty-five. Thousands turned out to watch as his casket was carried through the streets of New York City and placed aboard the ship that would carry him back to Sweden for burial. Every flag in the harbor flew at half-mast, and a fleet of monitors fired a salute.

It was all a way of saying—*finally and at long last*—

Thank you very much,
Captain John Ericsson!

John Ericsson Biography

John Ericsson was born in the center of Sweden in 1803 with a huge curiosity, an unshakable self-confidence, and the resilience to spring back from one defeat after another. As soon as he could hold a pencil, he began making careful drawings of the machines and tools in the mines where his father worked as a supervisor. He wanted to know how everything he saw worked. As soon as he knew how something worked, he wanted to make it work better. When he was five, he constructed a perfect little windmill out of tableware and pieces of a clock he'd taken apart.

At age seventeen he joined the Swedish army and was assigned to prepare maps, which were such works of art that they landed in the Swedish Royal Archives, where they can still be seen today. Still, John wasn't happy. Maps were fine and good but what he really wanted to do was invent things, and neither Sweden nor England (where he moved in 1826) appreciated his inventions. Everyone seemed to see his designs as impossible dreams. But John never wasted time chasing the impossible. In his view his inventions were practical, elegant, inspired, and completely possible. In 1839 he moved to New York City, hoping to find people who could understand that.

In New York he designed a warship that was completely made of iron. Most of the vessel, including the steam engines, the screw propeller that powered it, and the living quarters for the crew, were underwater. The only thing visible on deck was a round turret housing a gun that could revolve and shoot in any direction. It was equipped with "reflecting telescopes" (periscopes) and "hydrostatic javelins" (torpedoes). He sent his design to the emperor of France. Napoléon III was not interested, so John tossed his cardboard model in a box and moved on to other inventions. It was that rejected cardboard model, dusted off and shown, by chance, to a visitor from Washington, D.C., seven years later, that became the ironclad *Monitor*.

When the *Monitor* succeeded in protecting the Union fleet against the South's ironclad *Merrimac* at the Battle of Hampton Roads in 1862, John Ericsson finally received the recognition that had eluded him all his life. He also received orders for more monitors. That meant a steady income. And that meant he was free to do the one thing he always wanted to do: invent things. "I propose to continue my work so long as I can stand at a drawing board," he said. He died one day before the twenty-seventh anniversary of the Battle of Hampton Roads.

John Ericsson Time Line

July 31, 1803	John Ericsson is born in Langbanshyttan, Sweden.
November 23, 1839	Ericsson moves to New York City, where he lives for the rest of his life.
September 26, 1854	Ericsson submits a design for an ironclad warship to Napoléon III, the emperor of France. His design is rejected.
April 12, 1861	Confederates bombard Fort Sumter and the Civil War begins.
July 4, 1861	Gideon Welles, the Union's secretary of the navy, recommends the appointment of a "proper and competent board" to look into the construction of an ironclad warship.
July 11, 1861	Stephen Mallory, the Confederate secretary of the navy, orders the *Merrimac* to be converted from a wooden warship into an ironclad.
September 14, 1861	Ericsson signs a contract to build the Union navy an ironclad based on the design rejected by Napoléon III.

February 17, 1862	The Confederates change the *Merrimac*'s name to the *Virginia*. History has restored her original name.
March 6, 1862	The North's ironclad, the USS *Monitor*, leaves the Brooklyn Navy Yard.
March 8, 1862	The *Merrimac* arrives at Hampton Roads. She sinks the *Cumberland*, sets the *Congress* on fire, and damages the *Minnesota* before low tide forces her to retreat.
March 8, 1862 (evening)	The *Monitor* steams into Hampton Roads.
March 9, 1862 (morning)	The *Merrimac* returns to finish off the *Minnesota*. The Confederate crews spot a strange vessel directly in front of the *Minnesota*. The battle of the ironclads begins.
March 9, 1862 (midday)	The *Merrimac*, low on fuel, leaking, and experiencing engine trouble, steams upriver to Norfolk, leaving the North's blockade intact.
March 14, 1862	The U.S. Navy orders six additional monitors. Twenty-nine more are built during the Civil War.
May 10, 1862	The Union army storms Norfolk. The Confederates destroy the *Merrimac* to keep her out of Union hands.
December 31, 1862	The *Monitor* runs into a storm and sinks somewhere off Cape Hatteras, North Carolina.
March 8, 1889	John Ericsson dies at his home in New York City.
May 29, 1926	A monument to the memory of John Ericsson is unveiled in Washington, D.C.
1937	The last monitor, the USS *Cheyenne*, is retired from the U.S. Navy.
Summer 1973	A research team locates the sunken remains of the USS *Monitor*.

Bibliography

Adams, Scarritt. "The Miracle That Saved the Union." *American Heritage* 27, no. 1 (December 1975): 72.

"Back to His Land," *New York Times*, 24 August 1890, p. 1.

Church, William Conant. *The Life of John Ericsson*. New York: Charles Scribner's Sons, 1890.

deKay, James Tertius. *Monitor: The Story of the Legendary Civil War Ironclad and the Man Whose Invention Changed the Course of History*. New York: Ballantine Books, 1997.

Greene, Dana S. "I Fired the Gun and Thus Commenced the Great Battle." *American Heritage* 8, no. 4 (June 1957): 10.

Holzman, Robert S. "How Steam Blew the Rowdies Out of the Fire Departments." *American Heritage* 7, no. 1 (December 1955): 66.

Webster, Donald B. "The Beauty and Chivalry of the United States Assembled. . . ." *American Heritage* 17, no. 1 (December 1965): 50.

White, Ruth. *Yankee From Sweden*. New York: Henry Holt and Company, 1960.

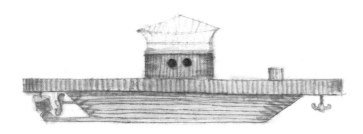

To three Ericsson family descendants:

Ruth Brouillette, Naomi Nordhielm, and Jeppie Harris III

C. N. W.

To my friend Chet Mills

A. G.

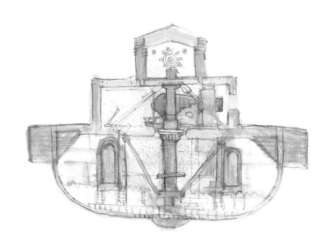

Text copyright © 2005 by Connie Nordhielm Wooldridge
Illustrations copyright © 2005 by Andrew Glass
All Rights Reserved
Printed in the United States of America
www.holidayhouse.com
First Edition
1 3 5 7 9 10 8 6 4 2

Library of Congress Cataloging-in-Publication Data

Wooldridge, Connie Nordhielm.
Thank you very much, Captain Ericsson! / by Connie Nordhielm Wooldridge;
illustrated by Andrew Glass.— 1st ed.
p. cm.
Includes bibliographical references.
ISBN 0–8234–1626–7 (hardcover)
1. Ericsson, John, 1803–1889—Juvenile literature. 2. Inventors—Sweden—Biography—Juvenile literature.
3. Inventors—United States—Biography—Juvenile literature. [1. Ericsson, John, 1803–1889.
2. Inventors.] I. Glass, Andrew, 1949– ill. II. Title.

T40.E8W66 2004
609'.2—dc22
[B]   2003068574

Designed by Yvette Lenhart